THE CHEMISTRY OF HAPPINESS

Banj Lawrence

<u>**Table of contents**</u>

The Ultimate Guide to Mastering Your Mind: Techniques for Achieving Success and Inner Peace."

Introduction:

Chapter 1: Understanding the Mind

Chapter 2: Mindfulness and Meditation

Chapter 3: The Power of Positive Thinking

Chapter 4: Overcoming Negative Thoughts and Emotions

Chapter 5: Setting Goals and Creating Habits

Chapter 6: Self-Care and Mindset Shifts

<u>**DEDICATION**</u>
<u>**To my family, I would like to devote my work. To ensure that I had access to a top-notch education from a young age, they instilled in me a passion to learn and a willingness to accept compromises. Additionally honored are my close friends who have stood with me through all of my academic years.**</u>

<u>Introduction</u>:

Welcome to "The Ultimate Guide to Mastering Your Mind: Techniques for Achieving Success and Inner Peace". This book is designed to provide you with practical and effective techniques for mastering your mind and achieving a more peaceful and successful life.

In today's fast-paced and demanding world, it can be easy to feel overwhelmed, stressed, and anxious. Many of us struggle to manage our thoughts and emotions, which can lead to negative thinking patterns and a sense of disconnection from ourselves and others.

The good news is that it is possible to master your mind and find a sense of inner peace and success, no matter what challenges you may face. By learning to manage your thoughts and emotions, cultivate positive habits, and shift your mindset, you can unlock your full potential and achieve your goals.

In this book, we will explore various techniques for mastering your mind and achieving success and inner peace. We will begin by understanding the mind and how it influences our experiences in life. We will then delve into the importance of mindfulness and meditation, visualization and affirmations, overcoming negative thoughts and emotions, setting goals, creating habits, self-care, and mindset shifts.

By using these techniques, you will learn how to manage your thoughts and emotions, develop positive habits, and cultivate a more positive mindset. You will gain a greater sense of inner calm, resilience, and confidence, which will help you to achieve your goals and live a more fulfilling life.

Whether you are struggling with stress, anxiety, or other challenges in life, the techniques in this book can help you to master your mind and achieve a more peaceful and successful life. We hope that this book will be a valuable resource for you on your journey.

Chapter 1: Understanding the Mind

Our mind is a powerful tool that shapes our experiences and influences the way we think, feel, and behave. It is the seat of our consciousness and our sense of self. Understanding how our mind works is the first step in mastering it.

Different parts of the mind: Our mind can be divided into different parts, each with its own function. The conscious mind is the part of our mind that we are aware of and actively use to think, reason, and make decisions. The subconscious mind, on the other hand, operates below our level of awareness and is responsible for our automatic thoughts, feelings, and behaviors. The unconscious mind is the deepest part of our mind and is responsible for our instincts, impulses, and drives.

<u>Types of thoughts and emotions that arise</u>: Our mind is constantly generating thoughts and emotions, some of which are positive and some of which are negative. Positive thoughts and emotions, such as joy, gratitude, and love, promote happiness and well-being. Negative thoughts and emotions, such as fear, anger, and sadness, can lead to stress, anxiety, and depression.

<u>How the mind influences our experiences in life</u>: Our thoughts and emotions shape our experiences in life. They influence the way we perceive and interpret the world around us, and they determine how we respond to different situations. For example, if we have a negative mindset, we may perceive challenges as threats and become overwhelmed and anxious. However, if we have a positive mindset, we may see challenges as opportunities for growth and learning.

By understanding the different parts of our mind and the types of thoughts and emotions that arise, we can begin to manage our thoughts and emotions more effectively. We can learn to recognize when negative thoughts and emotions arise and take steps to shift our mindset towards a more positive perspective. This can help us to navigate life's challenges with greater ease and resilience.

In the following chapters, we will explore various techniques for mastering our mind and achieving success and inner peace. By using these techniques, we can learn to manage our thoughts and emotions, cultivate positive habits, and shift our mindset towards greater positivity and resilience.

Chapter 2: The Importance of Mindfulness and Meditation

Mindfulness and meditation are powerful techniques for mastering the mind and achieving a more peaceful and centered life. In this chapter, we will explore the benefits of mindfulness and meditation and how to incorporate them into your daily routine.

Benefits of mindfulness and meditation: Mindfulness and meditation have been shown to have numerous benefits for mental and physical health. They can reduce stress and anxiety, improve mood and emotional regulation, enhance focus and concentration, increase self-awareness, and promote overall well-being.

<u>Types of meditation</u>: There are many different types of meditation, including focused attention meditation, which involves focusing on a specific object or sensation, such as the breath; open monitoring meditation, which involves being aware of and observing one's thoughts and emotions without judgment; and loving-kindness meditation, which involves cultivating feelings of love, compassion, and kindness towards oneself and others.

<u>How to practice mindfulness and meditation</u>: To practice mindfulness and meditation, find a quiet and comfortable space where you can sit or lie down without distractions. Begin by focusing on your breath, noticing the sensation of the air moving in and out of your body. If your mind begins to wander, gently redirect your attention back to your breath. You can also try incorporating guided meditations or visualization exercises to enhance your practice.

<u>**Incorporating mindfulness and meditation into your daily routine**</u>: To reap the benefits of mindfulness and meditation, it is important to incorporate them into your daily routine. This can be done by setting aside a few minutes each day to practice, whether it's first thing in the morning, during a break at work, or before bed. You can also try incorporating mindfulness into everyday activities, such as taking a mindful walk or practicing mindful eating.

By incorporating mindfulness and meditation into your daily routine, you can learn to manage your thoughts and emotions more effectively, cultivate a greater sense of self-awareness, and promote overall well-being. These techniques can serve as powerful tools for mastering your mind and achieving a more peaceful and fulfilling life

Chapter 3: The Power of Positive Thinking

Positive thinking is a powerful technique for mastering the mind and achieving success and inner peace. In this chapter, we will explore the benefits of positive thinking and how to cultivate a positive mindset.

Benefits of positive thinking: Positive thinking has been shown to have numerous benefits for mental and physical health. It can reduce stress and anxiety, improve mood and emotional regulation, enhance resilience and coping skills, increase self-esteem and confidence, and promote overall well-being.

How to cultivate a positive mindset: To cultivate your negative self-talk and patterns of negative thinking. This can include negative beliefs about yourself, others, or the world around you. Once you have identified these patterns, you can begin to challenge and replace them with more positive and empowering thoughts.

<u>Some techniques for cultivating a positive mindset include</u>: Gratitude practice: Take time each day to reflect on what you are grateful for. This can help shift your focus towards the positive aspects of your life and increase feelings of happiness and contentment.

<u>Positive affirmations</u>: Use positive affirmations to reinforce positive beliefs about yourself and your abilities. For example, "I am capable of achieving my goals" or "I am deserving of love and happiness."

<u>Visualization</u>: Use visualization techniques to imagine yourself achieving your goals and living the life you desire. This can help to create a positive mindset and increase motivation and confidence.

Surround yourself with positivity: Surround yourself with positive people, media, and environments that support your positive mindset and goals.

By cultivating a positive mindset, you can learn to manage negative thoughts and emotions more effectively, increase your self-esteem and confidence, and promote overall well-being. Positive thinking can serve as a powerful tool for mastering your mind and achieving a more fulfilling and successful life.

Chapter 4: Overcoming Negative Thoughts and Emotions

Negative thoughts and emotions can be major obstacles to achieving success and inner peace. In this chapter, we will explore techniques for overcoming negative thoughts and emotions, including cognitive restructuring, emotional regulation, and reframing.

<u>**Cognitive restructuring**</u>: Cognitive restructuring is a technique that involves identifying and challenging negative thought patterns. By questioning the validity of negative thoughts and replacing them with more positive and rational thoughts, individuals can change their beliefs and attitudes about themselves, others, and the world around them. Cognitive restructuring involves the following steps:

- **Identify negative thoughts**: Become aware of negative thoughts and beliefs that may be contributing to negative emotions.

- **Challenge negative thoughts**: Question the validity of negative thoughts and look for evidence to support or refute them.

- **Replace negative thoughts**: Replace negative thoughts with more positive and rational thoughts that are based on evidence and reality.

<u>Emotional regulation</u>: Emotional regulation is a technique that involves managing emotions in a healthy and effective way. By recognizing and accepting emotions, individuals can learn to regulate and express them in a constructive manner. Emotional regulation involves the following steps:

- **Recognize emotions**: Become aware of and acknowledge emotions as they arise.

- **Accept emotions**: Accept emotions without judgment or suppression.

- **Regulate emotions**: Practice healthy coping mechanisms to regulate and express emotions in a constructive manner.

<u>Reframing</u>: Reframing is a technique that involves changing the way in which an event or situation is perceived. By reframing negative situations in a positive light, individuals can change their emotional response to the situation. Reframing involves the following steps:

- **Identify negative perceptions**: Become aware of negative perceptions of events or situations.

- **Challenge negative perceptions**: Question the validity of negative perceptions and look for alternative ways to view the situation.

- **Reframe the situation**: Reframe the situation in a more positive light by focusing on positive aspects or potential opportunities.

By practicing these techniques for overcoming negative thoughts and emotions, individuals can learn to manage negative emotions more effectively, increase self-awareness and emotional intelligence, and promote overall well-being. These techniques can serve as powerful tools for mastering the mind and achieving a more fulfilling and successful life

Chapter 5: Setting Goals and Creating Habits

Setting goals and creating habits are essential components of achieving success in any area of life. Whether you want to improve your health, career, relationships, or any other aspect of your life, it is important to have clear goals and establish habits that support those goals. In this chapter, we will explore how to set goals effectively and how to create habits that promote success.

Setting Goals Effectively

Setting goals is crucial for achieving success. However, setting the right goals in the right way is equally important. Here are some tips for setting goals effectively:

- **Be Specific**: Make sure your goals are specific and well-defined. Instead of saying, "I want to lose weight," set a specific goal like, "I want to lose 10 pounds in the next three months."

- **Be Realistic**: Set goals that are challenging yet achievable. If your goals are too easy, you may not feel motivated to work towards them. If they are too difficult, you may get discouraged and give up.

- **Be Time-Bound**: Set a deadline for achieving your goals. This will give you a sense of urgency and help you stay focused.

- **Write them Down**: Writing down your goals makes them more real and helps you remember them. Keep your goals in a visible place, like on your desk or on your phone.

- **Review Them Regularly**: Regularly reviewing your goals helps you stay on track and make any necessary adjustments.

Creating Habits that Support Your Goals

Creating habits that support your goals is essential for achieving success. Habits are the behaviors and actions we do automatically, without thinking about them. By creating habits that support our goals, we make it easier to achieve them. Here are some tips for creating habits that support your goals:

- **Start Small**: Make small changes that are easy to implement. For example, if you want to exercise more, start by taking a 10-minute walk every day.

- **Be Consistent**: Consistency is key to creating habits. Do your new habit at the same time every day to make it easier to stick to.

- **Make it Enjoyable**: Find ways to make your new habit enjoyable. If you don't enjoy it, you're less likely to stick to it.

- **Hold Yourself Accountable**: Share your goals and habits with someone else and ask them to hold you accountable.
- **Celebrate Your Successes**: Celebrate each success, no matter how small. This will help you stay motivated and focused on your goals.

In conclusion, setting goals and creating habits are essential components of achieving success. By setting specific, realistic, and time-bound goals, and creating habits that support those goals, you can achieve anything you set your mind to. Remember to start small, be consistent, and celebrate your successes along the way.

Chapter 6: Self-Care and Mindset Shifts

Self-care and mindset shifts are essential for promoting success and inner peace. Taking care of yourself physically, mentally, and emotionally is important for maintaining your overall well-being, while adopting a positive mindset can help you achieve your goals and overcome obstacles. In this chapter, we will explore the importance of self-care, mindset shifts for promoting success and inner peace, and the benefits of positive self-talk and self-compassion.

Importance of Self-Care

Self-care is any activity that promotes your physical, mental, or emotional well-being. It is important for maintaining good health and reducing stress. Here are some tips for practicing self-care:

- **Prioritize Sleep**: Getting enough sleep is essential for your physical and mental well-being. Aim for 7-9 hours of sleep each night.

- **Exercise Regularly**: Exercise is important for maintaining good physical health and reducing stress. Aim for at least 30 minutes of exercise each day.

- **Eat a Balanced Diet**: Eating a balanced diet with plenty of fruits, vegetables, and whole grains is important for your physical and mental well-being.

- **Practice Mindfulness**: Mindfulness practices, such as meditation or deep breathing, can help you reduce stress and increase relaxation.

- **Take Time for Yourself**: Taking time for yourself to do something you enjoy, like

reading a book or taking a bath, can help
you recharge and reduce stress.

Mindset Shifts for Promoting Success and Inner Peace

Mindset shifts are changes in your perspective
or way of thinking that can help you achieve
your goals and overcome obstacles. Here are
some mindset shifts for promoting success and
inner peace:

- **Practice Gratitude**: Focusing on what you
  are grateful for can help you shift your focus
  to the positive and reduce stress.

- **Embrace Failure**: Failure is a natural part
  of the learning process. Instead of seeing it
  as a negative, embrace it as an opportunity
  to learn and grow.

- **Believe in Yourself**: Believe in yourself and
  your ability to achieve your goals. Surround

yourself with people who support and encourage you.

- **Let Go of Control**: Letting go of things you cannot control can help you reduce stress and focus on the things you can control.

- **Focus on the Present**: Focusing on the present moment can help you reduce stress and anxiety and increase mindfulness and self-awareness.

Positive Self-Talk and Self-Compassion

Positive self-talk and self-compassion are important for promoting a positive mindset and reducing stress. Here are some tips for practicing positive self-talk and self-compassion:

- **Focus on the Positive**: Instead of focusing on your weaknesses or mistakes, focus on your strengths and accomplishments.

- **Be Kind to Yourself**: Treat yourself with the same kindness and compassion you would offer to a friend.

- **Practice Affirmations**: Affirmations are positive statements that can help you shift your mindset to the positive.

- **Accept Your Imperfections**: Accepting your imperfections and recognizing that no one is perfect can help you reduce stress and increase self-compassion.

- **Forgive Yourself**: Let go of past mistakes and forgive yourself for any perceived failures. This can help you move forward and focus on the present.

In conclusion, practicing self-care and adopting a positive mindset are essential for promoting success and inner peace. By prioritizing sleep, exercise, a balanced diet, mindfulness, and time for yourself, you can improve your overall well-being. By adopting mindset shifts like practicing gratitude, embracing failure, believing in yourself, letting go of control, and focusing on the present, you can overcome obstacles and achieve your goals. By practicing positive self-talk and self-compassion, you can promote a positive mindset and reduce stress

Conclusion:

Throughout this book, we have explored various techniques for mastering your mind and achieving success and inner peace. We started by understanding the mind and how it influences our experiences in life. We then delved into the importance of mindfulness and meditation, visualization and affirmations, overcoming negative thoughts and emotions, setting goals, creating habits, self-care, and mindset shifts.

By using these techniques, you can learn to master your mind and achieve a more peaceful and successful life. It is important to remember that mastering your mind is a lifelong journey that requires dedication and commitment. It takes practice and patience to develop new habits and shift your mindset.

As you move forward on this journey, remember to be kind and compassionate to yourself. You may experience setbacks and challenges along the way, but these are opportunities for growth and learning. Use the techniques in this book as tools to help you navigate the ups and downs of life and stay focused on your goals.

Ultimately, mastering your mind is about finding balance and harmony within yourself. It is about learning to cultivate a sense of inner calm and resilience, even in the face of adversity. With the right mindset and tools, you can achieve anything you set your mind to.

We hope that this book has provided you with valuable insights and techniques to help you on your journey. Remember to be patient, stay focused, and trust in your ability to master your mind and achieve success and inner peace.

ABOUT AUTHOR

Banj Lawrence is a young, gifted writer with a passion for good literature and good story telling. Ever since he was a child, he has always loved to write. He feels either as a writer or a reader, he is never satisfied. His mission is to write stories that will leave a mark in the reader's mind. 99% of his stories are inspired by true events. Banj Lawrence, a budding writer, is married and blessed with anything a man can only dream of.